# THE GAME OF LIFE

# AND

# HOW TO PLAY IT

By

ERNEST BASIM ABDULLAH

# The Game Of Life And How to Play It

Copyright © 2014 by Ernest Basim Abdullah

Published by: Sheila Edwards Howard Publishing

The Game of Life
And How To Play It
By Ernest Basim Abdullah
Printed in the United States of America

ISBN: 978-1-4675-9846-0

# The Game Of Life And How to Play It

*You, a man of few words, have made the most impressive dissertation on living a high quality of life in as equally few words. "The Game of Life and How to Play It" is a welcome reminder for those who already know and it heralds in a new group of interested people who want to live a good life and they want to know how to do it without further delay. For those of seekers, this book provides the steps on how to achieve your goals and stay in integrity with your passions. Your wisdom is evident in the breath of experiences you share and the simplicity of 'following the rules' becomes a crystal clear path for success. I appreciate this tool for sharing with others on the road to greatness. Thanks*

*Claudette Redic*
*Founder of Cider Enterprise.*

*A great writer was asked, "What makes one Excellent?" Her reply was: 'Love of God, love of his people, love of the environment and love of self.' This definition fits E. B. Abdullah.*

*Dianne Abdullah-Smith*

# The Game Of Life And How to Play It

## PREFACE

As a young man growing up my mother, always gave instructions for when I talked to my sister, Joy Woods, on her phone. She told me to, "just say, 'Hi, hello and goodbye.' She knew that the conversation could go on for hours. My sister lives in Chicago and my mother had concerns about her phone bill. At the time, we resided in New Orleans, and she had a problem with us doing all of the talking and her being left with the bill. My mother has passed now, God rests her soul and Bell South was happy. One time we were talking about life and how people seemed to live so haphazardly. It was during one of these lengthy talks that I mentioned to her, that they did not know the rules for the game of life. Flabbergasted with that thought, a discussion on the rules for the game of life began. For the most part, this is the outcome of what was said back then.

In 1980, when this book was started, there was no e-mail, no FACE BOOK, no Twitter, in fact, no internet, no computers as we know them, not even cell phones. Technology, today, is very different from when I first started this endeavor almost 45 years ago. The things people engage in today were only dreams back then so the ideas and concepts presented then were in their baby stages. With the help of the Almighty, the old has been intertwined with the new, and we present this game in greater depth with the aim of increasing leverage.

## DEDICATION

This book is dedicated to my loving sister, Joy Ann Woods, who has inspired me on many levels. Thank you from the bottom of my heart.

To my daughter and granddaughter, this is given to you as a legacy of my life.

## ACKNOWLEDGEMENTS

Without any doubt I say, it was my sister whose powerful conversations lead to the impregnation of this idea. As I gave further incite into the process of producing this work, you might say, I had a mid-wife that aided me to push and give birth to this baby, and that is my Life Coach Janine Ingram. There is only gratefulness for my initial publisher Minister Joanne Meeks. Even with her mother falling seriously ill, she still gave attention to my fragile work and handed it over to Publisher J.D. Cooper who has made it into this masterpiece that you see today.

In these acknowledgements of gratitude, I cannot neglect to mention the inspiring words and reassuring gestures that Ms. Claudette Redic unknowingly gave me, she encouraged the attitude of STICK-TO-IT-NESS.

It is with sincere appreciation and gratitude that I say "Thank You" to Janine Ingram, author of *Born To Be Rich,* and Sheila Howard, author of Inspired By,

Memoir of a Church Girl, and Founder of Sheila Edwards Howard Publishing. You helped me take my dream of publishing my book to its reality.

The carrot on a stick or my "Why" and the main reason for doing this is to leave something for the most caring daughter and grand-daughter there is, to show their progeny- that 'Da' and 'Grandpa' did exist and was productive.

To all of you I give my highest gratitude and say, Thank You, Merci, Gracious, Danke, Kamsa hamida and Shukran.

Thanks to you my readers, may you continue to receive the eternal fountain of abundance that Almighty God has in store for you.                     E. B. Abdullah

# The Game Of Life And How to Play It

## CONTENTS

## INTRODUCTION
### *The Game of Life*

The bottom line is – GOD'S GOT YOUR BACK!

There is a bakery in New Orleans, Louisiana on North Carrollton Avenue near Earhart Boulevard. It has a sign on the outside wall which reads, "LIFE IS TOO SHORT. EAT DESSERT FIRST." Well, here it is, your dessert is served now.

GOD'S GOT YOUR BACK!

I was walking home from the store, in Chicago, and a businessman on the corner yelled at me, 'Loose squares, loose squares' (loose squares are single cigarettes). I smiled, shook my head and continued to walk, but he kept talking and his conversation drew me to him. He was saying that you had to be positive in your life and make every effort to do the right thing. He wasn't a preacher and then again he was. It was street preaching that only the ones with a sensitive ear could relate to. He let me go with this saying, 'God's got your back.' Thank you Mr. Lee.

I am not going to let you forget that this is the dessert. If you eat the meal first, without dealing with this dessert, you may be too full to get this down. Plus, I think it is more enjoyable this way.

The dessert that is served is a delicious peanut butter cookie – a peanut butter sandwich cookie. This treat has three parts to it. There are two cookies outside, and they are sweet. Then there is the creamy peanut butter substance on the inside that is salty. The first layer on the outside is, 'God's got your back," you like that? It is sweet and with good flavor. The other side of this cookie is 'I am a piece of the Master. That makes me a Masterpiece.' Now inside these two sweet things comes the salt. 'Everything God created is good' – spiders, roaches, caterpillars, noisy neighbors, in-laws, gang-bangers, bullies, men who like men, women who like women, niggers, spicks, redneck crackers... These subject matters are pretty salty I know, but remember it is coming between some really sweet stuff, 'God's got your back' and 'I am a piece of the Master. That makes me a Masterpiece.'

Against all of this salt, there is God your protector. Despite all of this, YOU are a Masterpiece, and this is a reality. These things are not salty to everyone. Some people 'love' spiders, roaches and caterpillars, and honestly, we may be the loud neighbors, gang-bangers and bullies. In many cases, some people hang with the niggers, spicks and rednecks. We all love peanut butter cookies. It is like mixing salty, nutty and sweetness all together and when we view life this way it taste better.

Salt is a preservative and when you focus more on the things that are unwanted than the things that really brings happiness, you are preserving the negative. Doing that keeps you stuck. In actuality, the salt is the added challenges that can cause you growth. If it doesn't kill you, it will make you stronger. These challenges are meant to be stepping stones to a better you. Each fear or discomfort that you give peace too; will elevate you in your humanism. It would be advantageous to stop trying to change the salt and start changing the way you allow the salt to affect you. Life is not about changing the things out there. It is about changing your heart, your thinking, and your actions which in doing so will give you better results in your life. 'Everything God created is good.' You are focusing more on the salt than the outside of the cookie – 'God's got your back' and especially 'you are a masterpiece.' What we focus on is what we give power to. If we focus on the salt, we give power to the salt. If we focus on the good, we give power to the good.

We have been programmed to look for the negative. We have inspections where the inspector is only looking for something out of place or some malfunction. We have test where the tester is only looking for mistakes. We can have 99.9% right and .1% wrong and we are considered lacking. If everything God created is good then why not look for the good? Looking for the good is looking for God in His creation. It is there. We have been trained to look for the negative and looking for the positive is going to be very difficult in the beginning, but it is possible. I heard a city councilman in Chicago say that this summer would be a violent one. She based this on one incident that happened in March 2014. So she predicted that the entire summer would be bad. She had her focus on the negative and therefore she chose to spread that negative power into the future. Why couldn't she say that this summer is going to be pleasant and peaceful and everyone will have a great time inside and out in the streets? I say that because last summer I heard many people profess to how terrible and devastating the winter would be because of how the summer months progressed. Yes, they called it. The winter of 2013 – 2014 was one of the worst in the history of the Chicago. Why not look for and expect the best? Why not look for and expect the good? We could possibly change the weather. All I'm saying is we expected the worst and got it. Let's try something different. Let's expect the best and see what happens.

Are you thinking that this is far out? Well, yes and no. I gave examples of people expecting the worst and the worst showing up as expected. However, there are many examples of people expecting the best and getting it. It is called faith. What's wrong with expecting good from God? God is your Master and you are a Masterpiece, Right? Then who is in charge of the weather? I mean, isn't it said in the Bible that He gave us dominion over this earth? Therefore, we have to understand that what we focus on is what we get. If we focus on being poor, that's what we'll get.

If we focus on being rich, that's what we'll get. If we focus on being stupid, that's what we'll get. If we focus on being the best, that's what we'll get. As my Muslim brother Darrell Williams, in Chicago, said, BE YOUR BEST AND HE'LL DO THE REST. It is God's agreement to man that makes it happen, not you entirely. When we are our best in upholding His commands, we get His best. God has given us through His DNA the discipline, the drive, the stick-to-it-tive-ness, the courage and all the necessities to be the best we can be in this life.

So, what is the reward for doing good? Receiving something good in return, and If it doesn't happen this year we try again next year. It is God's promise to us that life works this way and when you practice this, it will work. Faith has two major qualities and one of them is patience. People today are looking for instantaneous results, but we have to consider that for many years we were expecting the negative. Therefore, let us put in the same amount of years anticipating the positive.

Remember, this is just the dessert. Most people get seconds on dessert so you are encouraged to read it again. Study it, digest it and make it a part of you. Then you can get into the GAME and get the gumbo, jambalaya and other Creole dishes that are yet to come. Bon appetite!

# THE GAME OF LIFE

# AND HOW TO PLAY IT

By

ERNEST BASIM ABDULLAH

## THE NEED FOR RULES
*The Opening Move*

Simple Simon left with a few coins
and came back with more coins - but less money.
Can you imagine bees working more hours in the day?
and producing less honey?
Our intent in this chapter
is to help you see the need for rules and laws.
And 'best' of rules may need to be changed
because of unseen flaws.

Jails! Red lights! Guns! God gave us the Ten Commandments! That should suffice. For those of us that need more…

In 1975, we attended a teacher conference in Chicago. The facilitator gave us a scenario about a young man who was in a large room handling a spiked steel ball & chain. It was a long chain and he extended it to its fullest and began to swing it around his head. It never touched the walls, thankfully, for if it did, it would have destroyed them. Besides, there was no one else in the room. As soon as one person entered the room, he has to pull in his chain a little. If enough people came into the room, he has to put it up. We have to have some rules.

In my first year at Clara Muhammad School in New Orleans, I told the children this story and we decided that we needed some rules for the school. The children proceeded to make rules. They were good rules that made sense to them and to me. They were always a constant surprise to me.

If the children got it, I know that you got it. We need rules for protection, for organizing, for safety, for recreation ... we need rules for everything.

In a conversation with a Chicago gang leader, I questioned him about the rules of the gang. His grandmother had asked me to talk to him because he wasn't following her rules. To my surprise he informed me that his gang had 147 rules and everyone had to memorize them. I told him the same story that I told the school children. He was very sympathetic.

As a young adult, I had the experience of living under the law of 'to spare the rod you spoil the child.' Well today, if you don't spare the rod, you may go to jail. I can remember a time it was ok to beat your wife. They could not put you in jail for beating your wife. She was your property (an extension from a slavery concept). OK, not only do we need rules but with more knowledge, the rules will change. 1940's concepts are quite different from the concepts of 2010. The meaning of one word today may not mean the same thing tomorrow. The word 'free' to some people means chaos. To someone else, it means not having to work today. And another person might think of not being a slave. And still another might think of getting something for nothing. Because word meanings change we need to flow with the new meaning of the word or, as the Supreme Court does, search out the original meaning to keep the same spirit of the word, to keep the 'RULE' intact. Bottom line – We Need Rules.

# The Game Of And How To Play It

## THE NEED TO KNOW THE RULES

*Book Player Poem*

Ignorance of the law is no excuse.

That's what the government says.

And who made the rule of mustard on hot dogs

and not mayonnaise.

Knowing the rules is important advice.

To one who is left behind.

Especially when gambling like shooting dice.

You're not expected to be kind.

What's funny is a man with more experience than

money

met a man with less sense and more change.

The funny thing is when they meet …

EVEN EXCHANGE!

# The Game Of And How To Play It

Me: "Let's play a game of chess."

You: "I don't know how to play chess."

Me: "Come on, I'll show you how to move."

You: "OK." Even after you learn the moves you keep messing up.

Me: "No, you cannot do that; you lose again."

To play the game properly or if your goal is to win, you need to know more than just how to move, you need to know the rules and the strategies. This is not just true of chess but of all games. Is life a game? If not, why are so many people losing and other people winning?

Rules are necessary to get you to where you have to go. If your goal is to get to the sixth grade, you just follow the rules of the school and the classroom and then follow the rules in mathematics, language and reading. If your goal is to get to Chicago walking, riding or flying you're going to have to follow some rules to get there. A simple map may not be sufficient. You need to know the rules for reading the map. To get to your goal, you have to follow the rules.

We have rules at school and at work. The city has rules. The state has rules. The Federal Government has rules, The government has a saying, "Ignorance is no excuse for breaking the law." Life's rules are different. If you break Life's rules it's not a life sentence. Mercy and forgiveness are always available and can be obtained through a change in life style (or simply following Life's rules).

The religious leaders tell you scripture contains the rules of life. And they are so very correct. But because of our different capabilities, experiences, attentions spans and/or other idiosyncrasies, we miss or misinterpret many of the rules of life. In the Torah and Old Testament, we are given the Ten Commandments. Do we have to be told, "Do not steal", "Do not lie", and "Do not kill"? I guess so. It's still happening. These rules were given to a people who had trite belief and knowledge of the Rules. These rules were given to a savage people. Do you really have to be told to leave somebody else's wife alone? It's like the game of chess we talked about in the beginning. We know how to move but we are ignorant of the rules. So we keep losing. There must be a greater set of instructions than just how to move. What do intelligent people need to know?

The rich have a different set of rules than the poor. The educated have a different set of rules than the uneducated. Happy people have a different set of rules than the sad or mad people. And the healthy usually live by a different set of rules than the unhealthy. Poor people cannot afford to be healthy. Buying healthy food is a luxury in the poor neighborhoods. The common practice is to not put a Health Food store in their area. So you first have to travel out of your vicinity to get healthy foods. Then without the proper education, we make poor choices. Kelly Maclean, Reader's Digest writer, said 'going to Whole Foods is like going to Las Vegas. You go there to feel good and come out broke'. Healthy foods are not priced or positioned for poor people. A wise man once told me that you can take a fool and put him in a castle and he'll turn that castle into a dump pile. But you can take a wise man and put him on a dump pile and he'll turn it into a castle. We have got to know the rules.

## RULE ONE FROM THE BIBLE: BELIEF AND RESPECT FOR GOD.

*Active Defense*

An active defense may work out,

if you're not planning on winning.

Attack, attack is the winning plan

And start from the very beginning.

Following the devil is for those who do not believe.

Following God is what we want to achieve.

Taking God's medicine seems hard to swallow.

But when we don't obey Him, then who do we follow?

There are many references in the Bible meaning 'belief is the beginning of wisdom'. This is one in - Job: Chapter 28, verse 28, *"And unto man he said, "Behold, the respect of the Lord, that is wisdom. And to depart from evil is understanding"*. Respect of the Lord is the wisdom. But to show that you understand, you have to do some action --- 'depart from evil'.

# The Game Of And How To Play It

In counseling a group of students in the Upward Bound program at Tulane University, we presented to them a situation where you see people lying, stealing and killing, who say that they believe in God. These people will fight you if you challenge them on that fact. What is happening here is, there is a belief but it is shallow and not based in logic but based on emotion. Emotions tell us, 'if it's good to me, it's good for me'. Simple studies on alcohol and sugar have shown that they have negative effects on brain functions. If we seek the knowledge of a higher power, in time, if you are listening and with sincere desire and open mind, filtered through proper education, your awareness will increase. We will begin to see God in creation. As our knowledge and awareness increases, our belief in and understanding of Life's rules increase. In time, our belief turns into a "know".

When you stop believing that there are rules for life and you <u>know</u> that there are rules for life, your respect for Life and its rules have reached fruition. Because you see the rules in creation, your respect for creation has grown. You know that there is a creator of these rules.

The only apology here is in the simplicity of the explanation. The growth that is obtained from the shallow belief to the knowing does not come without a struggle. Your struggle must be sincere. Your search and research must be constant. Coming into belief is the hardest part of reaching our goal. What goal are we talking about? We are talking about the goal God gave to all of us ... SURVIVE. Survive physically, survive mentally and survive spiritually. God created the laws and gave us guidance on how to follow the laws. He gave us the sun, moon stars, earth, fire, water, air and even the other animals to aid man on his entrance. It is like God was saying, "You will survive." And let's define this word 'survive'. Survive does not mean to have enough just to get by. It does not mean having enough so you can eat every day or enough to pay your rent. Survive means to have enough so you can feed your family and ten other families every day. Survive means to have enough so you can pay your mortgage off and buy a house for some other needy family. Survive means your cup is running over. Survive means you have found that eternal fountain of abundance that Almighty God has prepared for us.

Again, BELIEVING IS THE HARDEST PART OF REACHING OUR GOAL.

The first step to wisdom is shown in our actions. It is shown in our deeds and in our attitudes and accomplishments. Faith is that which resides firmly in the heart and which is proven by deeds. Persistence is another way of proving faith. If we turn our beliefs into knowledge and our knowledge into deeds, the reward is a trip to paradise - paradise in this life and the next. But the first step is belief. The beginning side of faith is wisdom. Wisdom is associated with understanding. Knowledge is retaining facts. The ending side of infinite faith is TRUTH, The Sure Reality.

I know you thought this book was about how to be successful in the game of life and you want to get a lot of money and a new car. You want a family and a good life. Well what kind of win is that if you get all these things and don't get to heaven? **"Well I had a great time while I was there, but I am catching hell now."** No, we are talking about winning here and in the afterlife too. The first step to wisdom, is believing in God's Wisdom, is knowing and living like there is a God. If we were to get the knowledge of the world to acquire the wealth of the world without the belief in Almighty God, it would not benefit us long. "A fool and his money will soon part." The people who discovered how to split the atom were very knowledgeable. They could have ventured into many things that would have benefited mankind with that knowledge. Instead, the first thing they used it for was to create the 'atom bomb'. Getting knowledge is a step in being successful or winning the game but it is not the first step.

Who or what is this God or this universal system that we are believing in? We can all agree that He is the Lord of all knowledge. Everything that exist, exist because He put it in place and sustains it. He birthed it, aided its growth and monitored its decline. Every cell in our bodies is under His inspection and control 24/7. That is every cell in each one of our bodies - Each of the 6 billion of us on the planet – along with the animals and plants (that is insects and bacteria) – the living things and the inanimate objects. Now that is the planet earth. There are 7 other active planets in our Solar System and He has knowledge of all activities on each of these planets. Hundreds of more planets have been discovered and He has knowledge of all the activities on each of these planets. Did you know an astronomer said that there are more stars in the sky than there are grains of sand on the earth? God has knowledge of all activities in and on each one of these stellar objects.

He knows the thoughts that we have as soon as or before we are conscious of them. And each one of us has totally different thoughts going on at the same time and we change our minds often. And we are only talking about His knowledge and the things that we know about. How much more is there that we do not know about? Can we see the greatness in just making an observation concerning His knowledge? I have trouble remembering what is on my mind and no knowledge of what is on yours or anybody else's.

With all this knowledge, it is easy to see why there were many cultures that entertained many gods. It is easier to believe many had different parts of this knowledge and power rather than one. A god for the wind, the rain, the ocean, the sun the moon etc.

Your belief is only as big as your knowledge and understanding of the thing that you believe in. This is only a trite journey about His knowledge. We are not talking about control or power or mercy. We are only talking about the things we know that He knows – our limited view of the universe – our limited view of His creation. Keeping that in mind should foster great respect and awe for the one who holds this knowledge. The belief in this possessor of this knowledge should be seen in our actions. We should live with reverence and respect in every action we perform, knowing that, we are never alone. A simple definition of belief is faith. FAITH AND BELIEF RULES.

We'd like to end this little section saying that with so many distractions, it's easy to forget the overall presence and enormous awareness of the Almighty. So persistent practice is required, which introduces us to the next chapter.

## RULE TWO IS FROM THE PRINCIPLES OF AL ISLAM: PRAYER

*Centralization*

The difficulties of life are many

as we live from day to day.

One solution common to all religions is

– Pray.

We pray to review the promises He made.

We pray to remind ourselves what to expect.

We live our lives being the best that we can be.

So we can look in the mirror with no regret.


If you are earnest about your belief in a higher power, the next thing you want to do is talk to it. Reverend Landrum of the Ebenezer Baptist Church on South Claiborne Ave. in New Orleans, has a big sign inside the front of his church that reads, "SOMETHING IS BOUND TO HAPPEN WHEN YOU PRAY."

Why do we pray? And what is prayer?

Prayer is simply sending a message to the universe. But it is also a reminder to us of who we follow. It could be a message of gratitude for things we have. Or it could be a message being thankful for the things to come. It could be a message in acknowledgement of the simplicity, complexity and grandeur of His creation. Prayer is worship. The message of gratitude keeps you spiritually healthy. You are seeing the laws of the universe at work and you are grateful that these laws work in your life. First, we are grateful. Prayer is a reminder for us to be grateful.

Muslims pray 5 times a day. The only thing they ask for in their prayers is guidance, 'Show us the way of the obedient people'. If we really understand, we should be praying all day. That does not mean we should be on our knees all day. It means we should invite God to be with us in every action we do all day. We should be thanking God all day. We should be asking for His assistance all day. We should be acknowledging the beauty of His creation all day. Prayer is the natural next step after we have believed. While brushing our teeth, thank God for teeth. While riding a bike, thank God for legs. While in the wash room, thank God for a making a way out.

You are created in and of excellence. You are created in and of integrity. You are created with a piece of the Master. So you're a Masterpiece. When you produce with excellence and integrity, you are worshiping God. When you live with integrity and excellence, you are worshiping God. When you are living to be the best that you can be, you are living a God filled life - you are living a life of obedience – you are living a life of prayer.

Part of believing is to believe that the Universe talks back. Sometimes the answer comes back immediately and other times it takes a long time to come back. To be sure, it will come to you only when you are ready for it. And you get the message only if you are listening - only if you have an ear – only if you know its voice. And sometimes No Answer is a message also. If you are living a life of integrity, a life of excellence, you will find that your rewards are great. Please remember, our prayers are answered not only when we are given what we ask for but when we are challenged to be the best that we can be. Like any father, God will reward His child for their good deeds. What is the reward for good, other than good? Yes, He talks back. Yes, there is an answer to every prayer. If we believe that there is for us a fountain of abundance and that our cups should be running over then why do we short change ourselves in our prayers. We pray for enough so we can pay our rent. Why not pray to pay the mortgage off for the house with enough left over to pay someone else's rent. We pray for a dollar raise. Why not pray for enough money so you don't have to work. A Fountain of Abundance; Our Cups Running Over. "SOMETHING'S BOUND TO HAPPEN WHEN YOU PRAY!"

When Almighty God began creation, He spoke and there it was. In the Bible He said, 'Let there be …". In the Quran He only said, 'Be'. He spoke creation into being. The words we use in our conversations are also powerful. We create ourselves in our attitudes, our likes and dislikes, our prejudices and beliefs. We also create our situations and relationships with other people and the universe. When we complain abut how much we hate our job; we'll soon find that we are more disconnected from our job. When we talk about our problems without solutions, we'll find the problems get bigger. When we discuss the negatives excluding the positives, we'll always produce more negative. God created positives with His words. What are we creating?

I like the scenario about the mama and daughter who are cooking and the mama tells the girl to go and tell your brother to come inside and eat. So the girl goes to the front door and yells to her brother, who is riding his bicycle up and down the sidewalk because his mother says not to go into the streets. The daughter yells, 'Hassan, come inside.' Hassan hears her and keeps riding. As he passes again she yells, 'Hassan, come inside'. Hassan gets faster on his bike and continues to ride. The daughter retreats and tells her mother that Hassan won't listen and he's not coming inside. The mother looks the daughter in the eye and says, 'Tell him that I said to come inside.' The daughter goes back to the front and yells to Hassan, 'Hassan, mama says to come inside.' The brakes screech as Hassan stops to obey. The daughter went with the name of mother. She went with the power of mother. Think if we do things WITH the name of God and not IN the name of God. We do have it. Let's go with it. Are we thinking that we can do this? Then when we fail we say, 'I can't do this'. Know that failure is a part of the learning process. We did something wrong, that's why we failed. Try something different, change something or maybe you made a mistake somewhere. Remembering you have the power of the Universe can give you the power to continue.

You are not the God. You are a part of the God, so you have to reach another level of God to solve this particular problem. Don't give up, think, read, imagine. That's the hardest work ... Thinking, reading, and imagining. That's why so many people don't do it. Go with the power of God. If you remember Him, He will remember you.

# The Game Of And How To Play It

Lynn Johnson, from Chicago, saw a house on 87th street and loved it and said, 'That's my house.' She went to the house and saw that it was For Rent and she made an appointment and got inside. She told the owner, 'This is my house and don't show it to anyone else.' The owner told her that this was not her house. Two months later Lynn moved in. Definiteness of purpose always wins. CLAIM IT! Now that's a real player. "SOMETHING'S BOUND TO HAPPEN WHEN YOU PRAY!"

## RULE THREE: GET EDUCATED

*En passant*

Everyone knows that one plus one is two

and two plus two is four.

But every time we add it up,

they get less and you get more.

My son the soccer player,

uses a grass rake to comb his hair.

I asked him, 'Is it ignorance or apathy?'

He said, 'I don't know and I don't care.'


Do you think God wants a dummy following Him?

George Washington Carver had a sickness that made him physically handicapped, so he turned to developing his mind through studying plants. He was a God respecting man and he prayed to receive the secrets of the universe. God told him that he could not handle the secrets of the universe, "just study the peanut". He could have said study the stars but then he would have needed a telescope. God chose something that he was already prepared for, something in a field he was familiar with, something he would like to study anyway. He didn't choose a big thing. God chose a small thing that changed the way people dealt with their crops and benefited their health and wealth.

Adam was taught the names and essence of all things and how to describe them. He taught him nouns, pronouns, verbs, adjectives ...etc. God taught Adam intelligent speech and communication skills.

Jesus spoke many languages; He was able to speak to the educated and uneducated. He spoke the language of the rich and the poor. He spoke the language of the believers and the non-believers.

A Russian soldier was able to memorize a set of Britannica Encyclopedias in six languages other than his own.

There is a story of Almighty God giving talents (gifts or purposes in life) to some men. He rewarded those who increased their talents and degrade the one that ignored his God given talents.

The scientist Albert Einstein is said to have used only ten percent of his brain. That is ninety percent unused. Today's technology has shown that the capability is much greater than that. Would God give us such a great capacity if His desire was for us not to have a great knowledge?

It has been said, "The pen is mightier than the sword." Do we need war? Today, the person with the computer steals more than the person with a gun. There's also a saying, "The ink of a scholar is more precious than the blood of a martyr." Does this sound like a God that wants you to be a dummy?

Because people are the cream of His creation and deserve great respect, the magic words 'thank you', 'please', 'forgive me', 'I apologize' and 'excuse me', are in order. These magic words are a sign of intelligence for believing in God. It has been said that the only commandment that Jesus gave was in John 15" 12, 'Love ye one another'. Now try that on for size. It takes a big person to fill those shoes. That means no resentment, no gossip and back-biting, no lying and stealing. This is going to take a lot of educating and re-educating. The older we get, the more set we are in our ways. Re-educating is only as difficult as we think it is. For you re-educating may be difficult but not impossible. With the youth, we have a chance to start it out right and give the world a much needed third chance.

They say it was the 'Flood' that gave us a second chance. We have the tools and technology. All we need is the desire and we can make it happen. Educate them on the functions of the body, the mind and our spirituality. Show them how to progress in all areas and the means to obtain and the benefit of wealth. Clean and wholesomely feed their bodies. Give them examples of minds rooted in the light of logic but free to explore the infinite potentiality of the imagination. Teach them to love the light of day but also to embrace the darkness of the night that shows them the possibilities in the number of stars. Show them a heart and soul filled with love to share. BE THAT EXAMPLE FOR THEM. As much as we need prayer, we need education even more. It is a one two punch. One without the other, results in a deficit.

As a child, Thurgood Marshall, (former United States Supreme Court Judge) was a great student; 'academic wise'. He would finish his work in class before anyone else which made him engage in other activities which disturbed the class. Actually he was a gang leader in his community. When his mother had dinner ready, she went to the front of the house where there were well kept lawns and pretty houses all in a row and called his brother. Then she went to the back of the house by the open sewer canal and where the gangs hanged out and called Thurgood. Many times he was sent to the office because of his disturbing activities in class. MANY TIMES. And each time he was sent to the office, the principal would punish him by requiring him to memorize a section of the United States Constitution. There are many lessons we can learn from this little scenario.

1. children learn what we teach them … good and bad.
2. God rewards excellence.

3. With those earphones on our head we could become the masters of this universe like we're supposed to be. And changed the information that we are consuming, we could be that Master Piece..

4. What we learn as children is usually what governs our adult activities.

5. Success is a result of many little activities rather than one giant action.

6. Persistence is the mother of reached goals.

7. Words make people

8. Our brains are like computers. If you put garbage in, you get garbage out. If you put good in you get good out.

Just a few!

## RULE FOUR: DO SOMETHING WITH YOUR TALENT
*Decoy*


I read a book called Think and Grow Rich,

So I've been thinking.

I'm thinking he has my money and I got the book

and I'm just thinking ...

'Just Do It' said one athlete.

'Just do it and don't think.'

So Mike jumped in, obeying his friend,

And people watched him sink.


If you're still with us, you are believing and praying so you're learning to 'survive'. You are prepared for the problems of the world. What do you do next? That is it 'DO'. Do something. One definition of education is to get you to do what you have to do whether you like it or not. That definition is fine. I would like to think also that education is a way to find your God given talent that *you like* to fulfill your purpose and God's purpose for you.

People who complain about going to work have not found their talent or gift that the Almighty has given them. That is why having a job, is still being a slave. Entrepreneurs are free people. Your talent is always something that you enjoy doing. Your talent is not referred to as work. Sometimes your talent can make millions of dollars and sometimes you will just get by. But all talents are from God and are meant for us to serve each other. FIND YOUR TALENT, DO IT BETTER THAN ANYONE ELSE AND THE MONEY WILL COME.

Build it well, whatever you do.

Build it straight and true.

Build it clean and high and broad.

Build it for the eye of God.

Anonymous

Your talent may be being a good mother to your children (and other children). Your talent may be being a deacon in the church. Your talent may be teaching or researching or fixing computers or skydiving. Do you think Mother Teresa was happy with her job? What about the William sisters, do you think that they are happy playing tennis? The Summer and Winter Gold Medalists, do you think that they are happy with what they have done? What is your talent? Education will help you find out. Then, Do Something. Action without study is fatal; study without action is futile and useless. Knowledge will get you to the door but action is the key to get you in.

ON MONEY!

I know we've heard that money is the root of all evil. How about this: 'Being Poor' is the greatest crime you can commit against yourself.

| 1.     1862 | 1.     2014 |
|---|---|
| 2. Work set for amount of assigned hours. | 2. Work set for amount of assigned hours. |
| 3. Rewards are issued by discretion of the superiors. | 3. Rewards are issued by discretion of the superiors. |
| 4. Days off regulated by the boss | Days off regulated by the boss. |
| 5. Appropriate uniform or clothing designated by employer. | 5 Appropriate uniform or clothing designated by employer. |
| 6. Meals and break time not open for discussion. | 6. Meals and break time not open for discussion. |
| 7. Age for beginning and ending period assigned or until death. | 7. Age for beginning and ending period assigned or until death. |
| 8. Self-improvement education not a priority. | 8. Self-improvement education not a priority. |
| 9. Men think that they are superior to women. | 9. Men think that they are superior to women. |
| 10.    SLAVERY | 10. HAVING A JOB |

Entrepreneurs are free people.

## System #1: DO SOMETHING!
## SYSTEMS THAT WORK

*decoy*

Contrary to popular belief, and against the laws of mathematics, and discarding the rules of logic, "IT'S BETTER TO GIVE THAN TO RECEIVE." A friend told me this was a mis-translation. It should read, 'IT'S BETTER TO BE IN A POSITION TO GIVE THAN TO RECEIVE. I have no problem with that. In fact, that is what this book is all about, getting you in a position to be able to give. You can't give it until you get it. It is a promise made to us from the Almighty. Because God said it, that should be enough. It is a show of His mercy and beneficence. It is a reward for showing an appreciation for His creation.

What is the reward for good except good? Would you cherish the dollar in your pocket more than an award from the Almighty? Are you saying that you worked hard for your money and you should not have to share? Or are you saying it is a sign of wisdom to be stingy. I have heard it said that the greatest generosity is not to give a person some fish but to educate them on how to catch fish. And they will never be hungry again. One big blessing is that you are able to give. You do not give hand me hand-me-downs, leftovers, outdated materials. You give of the good you have that is above your needs. Who blessed you to get these things? Remember the scenario we went through with His knowledge. The same can be considered when looking at His possessions. There is no end to His possessions. What is the reward for good other than good? Logic doesn't work here. Neither does arithmetic. This other level is called Faith; mathematics on a higher level. Kind words and the covering of faults are better than charity followed by injury.

If you give time to your car, (wash it) it returns its beauty to you. If you give food to your lawn, it will look pretty for you. If you give time to books, it will return self-esteem to you. Giving has its own reward. God gives without counting. His blessing are innumerable – breath, heartbeat, sunrise, etc. I have heard of a wealthy person who was giving away 90% of his wealth. He was still a billionaire. Do not neglect getting your wealth. Position yourself to give. What have you given today? Whether you have one dollar or a billion dollars, you should share something. The rewards from the creator are better than any possessions you own right now. The Bible says that Solomon was the richest man of his day. As a boy, God gave him the choice of requesting anything that he desired. He asked for wisdom.

### System #2: WHAT GOES AROUND COMES AROUND

*Middle Game*

This has been said many different ways in many different languages. The meaning is always the same – What you do to someone will eventually come back to haunt you. That is not just the bad. The good that you do will return to you also. And because these are times of great change, the time it takes for it to 'come around' is more rapid. If you are watching the news attentively, you can see the fall of America's government. But if you are using your eyes and mind looking for the good, you can see the rise of the God's government. 'coming around'. There must have been a lot of praying people in New Orleans. There was no hurricane in over 20 years and in August 2004, we had a whole week of 60 degree weather ... IN AUGUST. What a merciful God. Thanks. *(Obviously this was written before Hurricane Katrina in 2005)*

Speaking of a recipient of the wrath of Hurricane Katrina, Hurricane Katrina was for me a blessing. I was in a rut in New Orleans and had no desire to change or improve. If you are not making progress, you are going backwards. I was not making progress. Having everything taken away from me made the knowledge and wisdom that had been drilled into me throughout my life 'come around'. Even in my backwards state I was still doing good for people. When I got to Chicago the blessings were coming so fast it was hard to handle them. I thought that I was being introduced to the finest people in the city. Everyone had a generous and helpful attitude. What goes around comes around.

## System #3: WRITING DOWN YOUR GOALS IS THE FIRST STEP TOWARDS MAKING IT REAL

### *Castling*

Writing down your goals introduces your goals to the sense of touch. At the same time you're looking at it so the sense of sight becomes involved. Reading it out loud will get your mouth or sense of taste into the action while you are listening to yourself. Four of your senses get involved just because you wrote it down and recited it. With these many senses working in unity, you will have engaged the brain in the activity of reaching the goal. It will summon all past experiences to aid in this endeavor. Last and surly no least, when you write it down in simple, clear, precise language, God knows what you want. And now you have His help. *Where there is no vision the people perish. But he that keeps the law is blessed.* Proverbs 29: 18. Keep your goals in front of you. What you keep your mind on is the direction that you will travel. Write you goals down recite and review them often and stay focused.

## System #4: IF YOU TAKE ONE STEP GOD WILL TAKE TWO.

*Double Check*

First of all, like the rest of this, you've got to believe to make it happen. Planning increases you success. Planning assures your success. When you plan, you are committed. When you do not plan, you are just wishing. The will to win is worthless if you do not have the will to prepare. Success is a planned event that takes discipline. Discipline is choosing what you want most in your life over what you want right now. When you believe good will happen, watch out, here it comes. If you believe bad will happen ... Ouch! The Wright Brothers did not believe in staying on the ground and got success in flying – planning, belief and discipline. Henry Ford did not believe in the bicycle as being the only means of transportation and invented the automobile – planning, belief and discipline. PLAN for tomorrow, for next year, for the next 20 years; but TODAY, live it like it is your last. The will to win is worthless if you do not have the will to prepare. Don't gamble. Live your life so that you end up where you want to be ON PURPOSE. You will find that when you take your first steps, you will get a little help. But the further you travel into your endeavor; the help will come from all directions: a phone call with some information, a newspaper, magazine or book with something that you've been looking for. Help may come and planning may change but be like a rock with discipline. That is why we need education.

Reading is one of God's gifts. Everybody can't read. Even the people who were taught, some of them still cannot read. If you can read and do not read, you are still ill prepared. We have been in the company of some people who study foreign languages and they were able to pronounce all of the word on the page clearly but they didn't understand anything that they were saying. Reading: is deciphering written signs or symbols representing meaningful utterances which are used for communicating. If there is no communicating, there is no reading. Some people do the same thing in their own language. Reading is a gift. Use it or lose it. One religious leader said that when he heard that if you took one step God would take two, he decided that he was going to break out and run. Now he really believed.

## System #5: ATTITUDE/MAGNETISM

*End Game*

- All limitations are self-imposed.
- If you believe you can, you are right. If you believe you cannot you are right.
- Your attitude determines your altitude.
- If you are an optimist, the sky is not your limit. The sky is where you begin. If you are a pessimist, the earth is not where you will stay. It is where you'll die.
- Obstacles are what you see when you take your eyes off the goal.
- A man's worth is no greater than his ambitions. It demands great effort in his strivings.
- An enthusiastic attitude beats money and power and influence.
- Enthusiasm is faith in action.
- You have got to have a dream. If you do not have a dream, then how are you going to make your dreams come true?

- The poor focus on obstacles. The rich focus on opportunities.
- The free spirited are stifled by a job. The low spirited find a job a place of secured peace.
- "The world needs changing", says the 'thinking' masses. For the powerful, 'Changing myself is changing the world.'

Look where you want to go. It will pull you there.

- Viewing of your goals should be a daily activity. Being there emotionally should be a regular activity. The greater the emotion the greater the results.
- Any increase in finance must be accompanied by an increase in knowledge.
- Thinking big attracts big results. Thinking small attracts tiny results
- Being bossed mentality. Or being the boss mentality.
- In one hand are your dreams. In the other are obstacles. On which will you focus?

- Confidence defeats doubt. Faith defeats disbelief. Love defeats fear.

- More credibility is gained by saying, "I do not know", than by being a 'know it all' full of BS.

- As short as life is, we make it still shorter by the careless waste of time.

- Impossible means I'm possible

- Proper thinking demands freedom (entrepreneur). No thinking requires you to just be there (on the job).

- To assure success in making a friend, approach them with two God given angels – a smile and a kind word.

- Winners talk about their choices. Losers talk about their circumstances.

The more you think about a thing, the more space it occupies in your mind. Because all matter is energy. The bigger this thing gets in your mind the more gravity will pull the real thing to us. The more we think about it, the more we are pulled to it. This is a law of a higher power and that it's not just luck or some other illogical explanation. If it is a conversation on something we desire then gravity will make it happen for us.

We are grateful to the universe for established laws that give us the ability to create our desires. It keeps us in awe as we unravel the complexity of its grandeur that is revealed in its simplicity. We achieve this with a constant conversation with the universe. That is why we can change the weather in Chicago and all over the world. If enough of us start thinking and saying 'Good days are here this summer', 'Great winters are in the forecast'. Instead of concentrating on the snow. Giving energy to the weather that we do not want is what we are doing.

It is like the universe is saying, 'That is all they talk about so I'll give them more of it. That is where their mind is so I will help the conversation along.'

# CHANGE

*Exchange sacrifice*

Do you have change for a twenty?

Or do you want to change my mind?

A change is going to come soon, they say,

And everyone will be doing fine.

Don't wait on change to come.

Be the change you want to see.

Changing is hard.

Not changing is worst.

Take the steps 1,2, and 3.

No one wants to die.

But we all want to go to heaven.

Everyone wants to be rich.

But that's steps 4,5,6 and 7.

Change doesn't always mean to grow.

And all black people are not black.

Change can be fun,

Change can make you run.

Here's change for your twenty back.

# WORDS:
# THE MESSAGE OR THE MESSENGER
December 26, 2011
*J'Adooube*

Much attention is given to speakers, orators, and messengers. Do we see how unimportant the messengers are when compared to the messages they bring? Men have been known to kill messengers because of the message that they bring. The message had the force. The messenger was not the source of the message. Nor was he in anyway the manipulator of its contents.

Sometimes we just do not like the messenger and we reject the message because of who brought it. The messengers of God were treated no differently. There are examples of this all through history from Jesus to Muhammad and even today in the pulpit, "I don't like him so I stopped going to his church." or "Do you see the way he dresses – he can't tell me nothing". We can learn wisdom, even if we but listen to one who is a drunk. Wise men and women have been rejected because they didn't fit the physical norms of a group. Sometimes it's a benefit to know the background of the messenger and sometimes it is not. But do not reject the message because of the messenger. Accept or reject the message because of the message content, not because of the messenger.

## WORDS CHANGE PEOPLE

For one to become a Doctor one must study the words of medicine. For one to become a lawyer one must study the words of law. For one to become a teacher one must study the words one must teach. Words Change People.

For one to become a good liar one must study the words of a liar. A thief learns from a thief. A drunk learns from a drinker. Words Change people.

Children who are encouraged and shown gratitude will have a high esteem and much confidence. While children who are defamed and degraded will be under achievers and nonproductive. Why? Words Change People.

I have been told the meaning of the word "Bible" in the original language is Book. The meaning of the word "Quran" means *something to be read*. Why? Because God knows, *words change people.*
The first revelation of the Quran says "Read". In the Bible it says, "In the beginning was the word". Because Words Change People.

Infinite communication is what makes man different from other animals. The original indigenous Americans communicated with smoke signals. Some Africans communicate with drums. The deaf or blind have their own method of communicating. In football, they communicate one way and baseball another. Man has had flag signals, telegraph, telephone, television and tell a woman. Infinite communication is what makes a man a man. Because 'Words' make people who they are. In the Arabic Language the word for baptize means the same as color or change. Baptism changes and cleanses people. In Christianity the water is symbolically the cleaner which is poured over or the individual is dipped into. In Al Islam as in Christianity knowledge is the changing medium and Muslims get baptized every Friday and Christians on Sunday at their prayer meetings - because Words Change People.

Man in his original state is pliable, receptive, agreeable, productive and is a doer of good. With these attributes, unhindered, the laws of the universe would be used and received with the precise understanding that they work like mathematics. The laws of the universe (scripture) is the science of survival for man. The words of Divine Scripture contain the greatest message of success for man because Words Change People.

Communication is valuable. Without communication there is no love. Without communication there is no agreement on issues. Without words describing ideas there is no communication. WORDS have the power of God.

God's words create light – so do human words. The light of in-sight, the new vision, "some things dawned on me". For things to change, you have to change. Words make people, change people, create light to trigger sight - help people see themselves in a better life, in a better position, just better. Words are like a light for your path way to show us where to go, how to live, how to be successful in every way. We must be the change we want to see in the world. Words Change People.

## WORDS CHANGE SITUATIONS

Living in the city of Chicago has exposed me to some extreme weather conditions. I never knew what below zero was until I got here. I had heard about it in the movies but this was real life and I was not ready for it. I brought it my sister's attention that most people were wearing black in the winter. Whoever was in charge of the black dye was making a lot of money. Much of talk during the summer (2013) was about the nice winters we have had the last few years and how this was going to be a ruff one. I would hear that so often. I was not feeling it. Why not keep this blessing going and have all our winters great. But just like they called it, just like they spoke it, the worst winter on record since the beginning of record taking. I believe without a doubt that they spoke this winter into existence.

Here comes spring and the talk is about how crime will go up; how people will be on the corners more and the gangbangers will be out. WHY DO WE LIVE EXPECTING THE WORST? My Brother Hassan in New Orleans always says, 'The best is yet to come.' He lives expecting the best. We speak into existence the very things that we do not want. Why not focus and give power to the things that we want? I invite you people of Chicago to try something new. If you keep doing the same thing and getting the same results that you don't want – why not try something new. Speak of the good that you want to see. My Coach teaches me affirmations. Speak your affirmations, what you want to see come into existence.

- I WILL MAKE TWICE AS MUCH MONEY THIS YEAR THAN I DID LAST YEAR.
- MY FAMILY LIFE WILL BE MORE LOVING AND FORGIVING FROM NOW ON.

- I AM HEALTHY, WEALTHY AND WISE.
- THIS SUMMER WILL BE THE MOST PRODUCTIVE SUMMER IN MY LIFE. THERE WILL BE PEACE IN THE STREETS AND LOVE WILL FLOW LIKE THE WATERS OF THE MIGHTY MISSISSIPPI RIVER.

You don't have to believe it but if you keep saying it consistently you will. And it is not like you are lying to yourself. You are telling the truth before it happens. With persistence and enthusiasm, it will happen. With passion and purpose, it will happen. Speak life and it will happen. Speak death and there it is. We have the power of life and death in what we speak. I know enough people in Chicago and all over the world will identify with this to make it happen. Words change situations.

School suspensions, school detentions and prisons are not working. Let's make a habit of love. Let's try something different. TRY LOVE!

# FREEDOM

## *CHECK MATE*

*The following acronyms are not from my head but from many of the books I have read over the years. I cannot remember where I got all of them from but they are not mine. They have helped me and I pray that they will help you.*

- Freedom is an inner awareness - a knowing that nothing can touch the truth of who you are. It is the 'I am" that is within you. It is by freedom that a man knows himself, by his sovereignty over his own life that a man measures himself. Elie Wiesel.

- Freedom and justice are twins. Sometimes we sacrifice some freedom to strengthen justice. Justice is a staple. Imam W.D Mohammed.

- F. A. I. T. H. = Full Assurance In The Heart – Nicholas James Vujicic. That's freedom.

- H.O.P.E. – Having Optimism when Pessimism is Everywhere – Nicholas James Vujicic. That's freedom.

- Love liberates – love yourself, people, creation... That's freedom.

- Just living in the U.S. doesn't mean that you're free.

- You can live in a church, that doesn't make you holy.

- You can wear a black tuxedo every day that doesn't make you a butler or an undertaker.

- Can you eat breakfast at Tiffany's? Walk in Sherwood Forest in England at mid-morning, eat lunch in the French Quarter in New Orleans and Dinner in India at the Taj Mahal – ALL ON THE SAME DAY ??? If that's your dream and you're not doing it - Then you're not free.

- When you follow your dreams, THEN YOU'RE FREE, and you give others permission to follow their dreams.

- When you list your dreams anyone can count them. But only God can count the number of people that you've aided to be free by you following your dreams.

- You cannot lift a man up without rising with him.

- Live out of the glory of your imagination not out of the tragedies in your memories.

- If money is your only hope for independence, you will never have independence. The only real security that a person can have in this world is in accumulating the right knowledge. - Minister Louis Farrakhan

- Everything that God has done for us was done out of love. Why should we be different?

- Freedom is being your own boss.

- The opposite of earned success is learned helplessness.

- An acronym for spelling POOR: Passing Over Opportunities Regularly – King Solomon (Chicago)... learned slavery.

- Having a job is mental slavery.
- SELF HATE is a form of mental slavery resulting in crime, violence and poverty.
- You cannot hold a man down without staying down with him.
- Minding your own business is freedom
- The person who minds nobody's business but his own is probably a millionaire.
- Forgiveness is freedom.
- Forgiving comes in prayer. Being forgiven is the result of change.
- Talents are not rare. People who perfect them are.
- The first to apologize is the bravest. The first to forgive is the strongest. The first to forget is the happiest.
- Do not aim at things you really do not want.
- Do not speak words you will regret.
- Do not pass by opportunities to do good.

- F.E.A.R. = false evidence appearing real – Jim Winner - fear is slavery.
- Time is life. The way we spend our time is the way we spend our life. Be productive.
- Time is a limited allotment in our life and the real problem we have is how to live successfully within our limited time and space. Solve that and - THAT'S FREEDOM

How much money is a long lasting friendship worth? How much money is a great family relationship worth? Can we put a value on the relationship of business partners who show each other love and respect in a humane atmosphere? It is these kinds of relationships that we find the true wealth in successfully playing the game of life.

Again, we thank you again for your patience in reading this book. And in closing, we pray, this has helped someone. We thank Him for our successes and our failures. For we know it has helped us. And we know it took all of that to make us the person we are today.

## PRAYER

God – There is no god but Him. He is the ever living, the self-subsisting and the fountain of life for all beings. No slumber or sleep can overtake Him. For Him are all things in the heavens and the earth. Is there anyone who can intercede in His presence except with his permission? He knows what comes before and after and no one can share His knowledge except as He wills. His throne extends over the heaven and the earth, and He feels no fatigue in preserving them both, for He is the Most High, The Great. *The Quran, Chapter 2: 255.*

# The Game Of And How To Play It

Except for the Ten Commandments, many people are unaware of rules for guiding their lives. They live solving their problems daily, hourly or by the minute. Not being conscious of the rules is like trying to watch an unfamiliar game from the sidelines; then somebody tells you that you lose. If you do not know the rules, you could not know that you are in a game. The fact that there are poor people and rich people tells you that someone is winning and someone is not. Can we first accept the fact that life is a game? Then there must be rules. Life may be complicated but the rules are simple. The complexity enters with our thinking, our cultures, or our way of life. When we can break free of those barriers, following the rules is simple. We win by playing the game.

Jeanne Marie and Gram-pa

**You have to learn the rules of**
**"the game"**
**THEN**
**you have to**
**play better than anyone else.**

ALBERT EINSTEIN

وَٱلْكَٰفِرُونَ هُمُ ٱلظَّٰلِمُونَ ۞ ٱللَّهُ لَآ إِلَٰهَ إِلَّا
هُوَ ٱلْحَىُّ ٱلْقَيُّومُ لَا تَأْخُذُهُۥ سِنَةٌ وَلَا نَوْمٌ لَّهُۥ مَا فِى
ٱلسَّمَٰوَٰتِ وَمَا فِى ٱلْأَرْضِ مَن ذَا ٱلَّذِى يَشْفَعُ عِندَهُۥٓ إِلَّا بِإِذْنِهِۦ يَعْلَمُ
مَا بَيْنَ أَيْدِيهِمْ وَمَا خَلْفَهُمْ وَلَا يُحِيطُونَ بِشَىْءٍ مِّنْ عِلْمِهِۦٓ إِلَّا
بِمَا شَآءَ وَسِعَ كُرْسِيُّهُ ٱلسَّمَٰوَٰتِ وَٱلْأَرْضَ وَلَا يَـُٔودُهُۥ حِفْظُهُمَا
وَهُوَ ٱلْعَلِىُّ ٱلْعَظِيمُ ۞ لَآ إِكْرَاهَ فِى ٱلدِّينِ قَد تَّبَيَّنَ ٱلرُّشْدُ مِنَ ٱلْغَىِّ

Prayer in Arabic language from page 63